Tommy and The Feeling Factory
By Chris Horne

Chapter 1: The Storm Inside

Tommy sat on his bed, staring at the floor. His football boots lay beside him, still covered in mud from today's match. He should have been happy — his team had won — but instead, a tight knot twisted in his stomach.

All he could think about was the goal he let in.

It played over and over in his mind: the ball flying towards him, his dive just a second too slow, the sting of watching it hit the back of the net. He had made some incredible saves that day, but none of that seemed to matter.

"I always mess up," he muttered under his breath, kicking at the floor in frustration.

Just then, his dad knocked on the door and stepped inside. "Tough game?" he asked.

Tommy nodded, still staring down. "I can't stop thinking about that goal I let in. If I'd just reacted faster, we wouldn't have conceded."

His dad sat down beside him. "That's football, Tommy. Even the best goalkeepers in the world let in goals."

Tommy sighed. "Yeah, but I can't stop feeling bad about it."

His dad smiled knowingly. "You know, there's a way to change how you feel about that. Let me tell you about something called the Feeling Factory."

Tommy looked up, curious. "What's that?"

His dad tapped the side of his head. "It's in here. Imagine a huge factory inside your mind. There are workers in there, sorting through your thoughts and feelings, deciding which ones to focus on."

Tommy frowned, intrigued despite himself. "Like little people running around inside my brain?"

His dad chuckled. "Sort of! And sometimes, those workers get things wrong. They focus too much on the bad stuff, like a single mistake, and ignore all the good things you did. But the good news is… you can train them to do a better job."

Tommy sat up a little. "How?"

His dad winked. "You'll see. Why don't you visit the Feeling Factory yourself?"

Before Tommy could ask what he meant, a strange sensation washed over him. It was like he was floating—not asleep, not awake, but somewhere in between. His room began to blur, colours swirling together like paint in water.

Then …

A soft whoosh filled his ears.

And suddenly, everything changed.

Chapter 2: Welcome to the Factory

Tommy blinked, rubbing his eyes. He couldn't believe what he was seeing. One moment, he'd been in his room feeling upset about the game, and the next, he found himself standing in front of a towering building. The words "The Feeling Factory" were boldly painted across the front in large, bright letters. Steam billowed from chimneys, and enormous gears turned behind the factory's windows. Conveyor belts whizzed by, carrying glowing orbs of different colours and shapes, each one looking more mysterious than the last.

Tommy's mouth dropped open. "What… what is this place?"

A man in a dazzling green coat appeared, a wide smile on his face. He had a warm, friendly look about him, with bright eyes and an air of excitement. "Ah! Tommy! Welcome! I'm Mr. Cooper, the head of the Feeling Factory."

Tommy took a step back, feeling a bit dizzy. "This is… inside my head?"

Mr. Cooper chuckled. "That's right! All the emotions you feel are made right here. The Feeling Factory is where your mind works to create feelings for you to experience. But, sometimes, things get a little… well, messy." He waved his hand towards a large open door.

Tommy squinted, peering inside. The room beyond was bustling with activity. Workers were running in every direction, their faces flushed with urgency. They were tossing bright red, spiky "frustration balls" onto moving conveyor belts. The balls bounced and jostled, almost as if they were alive, their sharp edges glowing like embers in a fire.

"This is where your frustration is created," Mr. Cooper explained, pointing to the chaos. "It's a bit out of control in here right now. We get a lot of those kinds of feelings when things don't go as planned, like missing an important save."

Tommy's eyes widened. He could feel the heat of the frustration balls even from where he stood. "So… all those feelings I had after the game — about missing that save — are coming from this place?"

"Bingo!" Mr. Cooper said, grinning. "But don't worry. This place doesn't just make the emotions—it also helps you learn how to manage them. With the right tools, we can fix the mess, change the way you feel, and make everything work the way you want it to."

Tommy looked around, still in awe. There were rooms off to the side with different types of emotions floating around in jars—some with peaceful blue orbs, others with bright yellow ones, and even some with purple, swirling, dream-like shapes. There was a large, colourful control panel, with buttons that seemed to correspond to different feelings. Tommy couldn't help but feel excited. This was the kind of adventure he hadn't expected, but it felt like the perfect way to figure out how to feel better.

Mr. Cooper tapped Tommy's shoulder. "Come on, let me show you how we can clean things up. Ready to learn how to control your emotions?"

Tommy took a deep breath, his mind buzzing with possibilities. "Yes! I'm ready!"

Chapter 3: See the Big Picture

Mr. Cooper smiled warmly and gestured towards a large, shiny control panel that appeared in the middle of the room. "This is where the magic happens, Tommy. It's called reframing. We can use it to help you see the big picture and feel better about your experiences. Let's start with that memory of missing the save in the match."

Tommy hesitated, feeling that familiar knot in his stomach when he thought about the missed save. The moment appeared on a giant screen in front of him, the ball flying past him and into the net. Tommy winced as he watched himself fall short.

"See, that's what happens when we only focus on one small moment," Mr. Cooper explained. "But what if we zoomed out and looked at the whole game? What if we took a step back and considered everything you did?"

Tommy furrowed his brow. "What do you mean?"

Mr. Cooper clicked a button on the panel, and the screen flickered, showing a different scene. This time, it zoomed in on Tommy making an incredible diving save, stopping the ball with perfect timing. Then, another save popped up—Tommy stretching out to catch a high ball with both hands. The screen continued cycling through moments where Tommy had played really well during the match.

"Do you remember these?" Mr. Cooper asked.

"Yes, Tommy said, I made some good saves and I helped my team stay in the game."

"And that's something to be proud of," Mr. Cooper said with a nod. "Now, think about this: what if you chose to focus on these great moments instead of the missed goal? What if you decided that those awesome saves were what really mattered?"

Tommy thought hard. He could almost feel the rush of pride that came with each save, the feeling of being in control. It made him feel stronger.

"You see, Tommy," Mr. Cooper continued, "it's not about pretending the mistake didn't happen. It's about choosing to focus on the big picture—the things you did well. When you do that, the mistakes lose their power over you."

Tommy's eyes brightened as he absorbed this new way of thinking. "So, I don't have to let the mistake ruin everything?"

"Exactly!" Mr. Cooper said, his eyes twinkling. "You control your thoughts. You can choose to see the big picture, focusing on your strengths and successes."

Tommy grinned, a huge weight lifting from his shoulders. "That actually helps! I think I can look back at the game and be proud of all the good things I did!"

Mr. Cooper smiled proudly. "That's the spirit. Remember, you can reframe anything in your life. It's not about pretending things didn't happen—it's about choosing to focus on what helps you grow and feel good."

Tommy stood taller, feeling like he could face anything now. He had learned a powerful tool—and he couldn't wait to use it in his next match.

Chapter 4: The Magic Box Trick

Mr. Cooper led Tommy down a winding hallway and into a new room. This one was soft and peaceful, with a big window letting in the sunlight. There were no distractions, just quiet and calm.

"Sometimes, Tommy," Mr. Cooper said, "we hold onto bad feelings—like frustration, disappointment, or even anger. And when we do, those feelings can make us feel heavy, like we're carrying a big backpack of rocks around all the time. But there's a way to let go of those feelings, to release them and move forward."

Tommy gave a gentle nod, but he was still unsure. "But how do you get rid of them?"

Mr. Cooper smiled and gestured to an empty space in the room. "It's actually simpler than you think. I'm going to teach you something called the Magic Box Trick. It's a way to take those negative emotions, put them in a magical box and throw them far away, so they don't control you anymore."

He held out his hands. "I'm going to give you an invisible magic box. Take it."
Tommy reached forward and imagined holding a small box in his hands. It felt light but solid.

"Now," Mr. Cooper said softly, "close your eyes for a moment. Take a deep breath and think about the feelings you've been carrying with you—maybe it's frustration from a mistake you made, disappointment from something that didn't go right, or even worry about what might happen next. All of those feelings—gather them up, and put them in the box. Imagine each feeling going inside, one by one."

Tommy closed his eyes and focused. He thought about the time he missed an important save in the football match, the frustration that followed, and the worry about how others might see him. He imagined all of those feelings—heavy and dark—fitting inside the box, filling it up until it felt full.

When he opened his eyes, Mr. Cooper was smiling. "Now that the box is full, we're going to make it smaller. Slowly, shrink the box down—smaller and smaller, until it's the size of a dice."

Tommy imagined it. He could almost feel the box getting lighter and lighter as it shrank, until it was no bigger than a tiny cube in his hands.

"Good," Mr. Cooper said. "Now, here comes the important part. We're going to throw that box away—far, far away. Imagine yourself tossing it into the distance, so far that it becomes smaller and smaller, until you can't see it anymore."

Tommy clenched his fist and, with all his might, he threw the box into the air. He watched as it got smaller and smaller, vanishing into the sky until there was nothing left but the lightness in his chest.

A feeling of calm washed over him. His shoulders relaxed, and he took a deep breath, realising he felt… free.

"That was amazing!" Tommy said, his voice full of wonder. "I feel so much lighter! It's like all that frustration and worry just… disappeared."

Mr. Cooper smiled, his eyes twinkling. "Spot on, Tommy. By putting those feelings in the magic box and letting them go, you've taken control of them instead of letting them control you. And remember, you can use the Magic Box Trick anytime you need to let go of bad feelings. The magic box is always there, ready for you."

Tommy smiled, feeling proud of himself. He had learned something powerful—something he could use to help him feel better, no matter what happened in his day.

"Thanks, Mr. Cooper," Tommy said, his confidence growing. "I think I can do this."

Mr. Cooper patted him on the back. "I know you can. And you don't have to carry those heavy feelings around anymore. You're in charge of what you focus on."

Tommy left the room feeling lighter, like a weight had been lifted from his shoulders. He was ready for whatever came next, knowing that he could always use the Magic Box Trick to keep his mind clear and his heart light.

Chapter 5: The Power of Your Imagination

After Tommy's success with the Box Technique, Mr. Cooper led him down another hallway, the walls now lined with vibrant images of athletes in motion. Tommy could feel his excitement building, wondering what new adventure awaited him next.

They entered a room that seemed to shimmer with light. In the centre of the room was a large screen, and Mr. Cooper's eyes sparkled as he motioned for Tommy to sit down.

"Now, Tommy, I'm going to show you something that can make a big difference in how you play: visualisation. It's like creating a movie in your mind where you can see yourself doing amazing things. It helps you believe you can do them in real life."

Tommy's eyes widened. "You mean I can actually see myself playing better?"

"Absolutely!" Mr. Cooper said, smiling. "Visualisation is a powerful tool. When you imagine yourself doing something successfully, your brain doesn't know the difference between what's real and what you're imagining. It prepares you to do it for real, and it boosts your confidence."

Tommy was eager to learn more. "How do I do it?"

Mr. Cooper pointed to the screen in front of them. "Let's try it. Picture yourself in a football match — see yourself standing in goal, The ball comes towards you, and you're ready. You feel calm, focused, and confident. Can you see it?"

Tommy nodded. He closed his eyes, imagining the stadium around him, the crowd cheering, and the ball flying towards him. He could feel his hands tighten around the gloves, his body moving into position. He imagined himself jumping high into the air, catching the ball perfectly with a firm grip.

"Good," Mr. Cooper said. "Now, focus on the details. What does the ball look like? How does it feel as you catch it? Can you hear the sound of the ball hitting your gloves?"

Tommy did just that. He visualised the ball's smooth surface, the slight bounce as it hit his gloves, and the satisfying sound of it landing safely in his hands. He even felt the excitement in his chest as he made the save, hearing the roar of the crowd and feeling the rush of pride.

Mr. Cooper stood beside him, watching closely. "Now, Tommy, picture the whole sequence in your mind. You're watching it happen. Can you see it clearly?"

Tommy opened his eyes and smiled. "I can see it all! It feels so real!"

"That's the power of visualisation," Mr. Cooper said. "The more vivid you make the image in your mind, the more real it becomes. You're not just imagining the save; you're training your body and your mind to make it happen. Your brain will begin to believe that you've already done it — and when the time comes in a real game, your confidence will be there, ready to help you perform."

Tommy's heart raced as he thought about using visualisation before his next match. "So, if I imagine making lots of saves before a game, I can do it for real?"

"That's the power of the mind!" Mr. Cooper said. "Visualisation doesn't just help with sports. It works for anything you want to do. Whether it's playing football, giving a speech, or even taking a test, if you can visualise yourself succeeding, you're more likely to do it. The more you practice, the easier it becomes."

Tommy's mind was buzzing with excitement. He thought back to all the times he had doubted himself on the field—when he was unsure about making a save or felt like he might miss. But now, with the power of visualisation, he could picture himself doing better, feeling confident, and succeeding.

"It's like practising in my mind!" Tommy said. "I can see myself doing it before I even try!"

"Excellent," Mr. Cooper said, his voice full of encouragement. "And the best part is that you can practice anytime, anywhere. You don't need a football field to visualise. Just close your eyes, take a deep breath, and see yourself doing what you want to do—perfectly."

Tommy felt a sense of pride growing inside him. He knew that from now on, before every match, he would use visualisation to imagine making incredible saves and playing his best game ever.

"Thanks, Mr. Cooper!" Tommy said, his excitement palpable. "I can't wait to try it out."

Mr. Cooper gave him a friendly pat on the back. "You've got this, Tommy. Visualisation is one of the most powerful tools you have. Remember, success always starts in your mind. If you can picture it, you can achieve it."

As Tommy made his way out of the room, his mind was alive with new possibilities. He was ready to put what he had learned into practice, confident that with visualisation, he had the power to face any challenge, and become the goalkeeper he'd always dreamed of being.

Chapter 6: The Power of Anchoring

Mr. Cooper led Tommy into a new room inside the Feeling Factory. The walls were lined with glowing buttons, each a different colour.

"This," Mr. Cooper said, "is the Anchoring Room. It's where you can store positive feelings and bring them back whenever you need them!"

Tommy raised an eyebrow. "How does that work?"

Mr. Cooper smiled. "Think about a time when you felt unstoppable—when you were completely confident and happy."

Tommy thought for a moment. "Oh! Last month, I saved a penalty in the final minute of a match! Everyone cheered, and I felt amazing!"

"Perfect!" Mr. Cooper clapped. "Now, let's anchor that feeling. Close your eyes and step into that memory. See what you saw, hear the sounds, feel that confidence rushing through you."

Tommy closed his eyes and imagined the moment—the roar of the crowd, the feeling of triumph as he dived and saved the shot. A huge smile spread across his face.

"Good! Now, as that feeling gets stronger, press your thumb and forefinger together—like this." Mr. Cooper demonstrated by pressing his fingers together. Tommy copied him, still lost in his memory.

"Now, open your eyes," Mr. Cooper said. "That feeling is anchored to that gesture. Want to test it?"

Tommy nodded.

"Okay, shake it off. Think about something else—like… what you had for breakfast."

Tommy thought for a second. "Uh… toast?"

"Good. Now, press your thumb and forefinger together again."

Tommy did—and suddenly, the confidence came rushing back! It was like he was back on the pitch, saving that penalty.

His eyes widened. "Whoa! That's amazing!"

Mr. Cooper grinned. "Now, anytime you need a boost of confidence, just press your fingers together. You've trained your brain to bring back that feeling instantly."

Tommy bounced on his feet, excited. "I can use this before my next match! Or even in school if I feel nervous!"

"Absolutely," Mr. Cooper said. "Anchors work anywhere. The more you practice, the stronger they get."

Tommy beamed. He had just discovered a secret weapon—a way to control his emotions in an instant.

Chapter 7: The Power Flick

Mr. Cooper smiled, sensing Tommy's curiosity. "Alright, Tommy. Now, let's work on replacing those bad thoughts with good ones. It's time to learn the Power Flick."

Tommy looked at the screen in front of him, which showed the moment he had missed the save. He shuddered a little, remembering how disappointed he had felt in that moment.

"Sometimes, when we have a bad thought or memory, it keeps popping up in our mind, and we can't stop thinking about it," Mr. Cooper explained. "But with the Power Flick, we can change that bad image and replace it with something much better."

Tommy rubbed his hands together, ready to try it out.

"Let's start by focusing on that bad image—the one where you miss the save. Close your eyes for a moment and really picture it," Mr. Cooper said.

Tommy shut his eyes, bringing the memory of the missed save into his mind. He could see the ball flying towards him and hear the sound of it slipping through his fingers.

"Got it?" Mr. Cooper asked.

"Yes," Tommy replied, frowning. "I see it."

"Good. Now, let's make a new image," Mr. Cooper continued. "Imagine yourself doing the exact opposite. Picture yourself diving for the ball, feeling strong and confident, and making the save perfectly."

Tommy pictured himself this time—flying through the air with perfect timing, his hands reaching out and catching the ball with ease. He could feel the satisfaction and excitement as he made the save, hearing the cheers of the crowd.
"Great!" Mr. Cooper said. "Now, here's the fun part. You're going to 'Flick' the bad image away. Picture the bad image shrinking down, getting smaller and smaller, until it's just a tiny dot. Then, *flick!* —replace it with the good image, the one where you made the save."

Tommy smiled as he imagined the bad image shrinking down like a tiny speck of dust. He then imagined the good image taking over, getting bigger and brighter, until all he could see was the perfect save, he had visualised.

"Flick!" Tommy said aloud, feeling a rush of excitement.

"Nice job!" Mr. Cooper said, clapping his hands. "Now, each time that bad image comes back, you can do the same thing. You can shrink it and swap it for a new, positive image. The more you practice, the quicker you'll be able to replace those bad thoughts with good ones."

Tommy's face lit up with a grin. "That's awesome! I can do that anytime I want, right?"

"Anytime Tommy!" Mr. Cooper said. "Whenever a negative thought or memory pops up, just use the Power Flick. Replace it with something that makes you feel confident and positive. The more you practice, the easier it gets."

Tommy gave a confident smile. He was already thinking about how he could use this technique the next time he was on the field, when a negative thought might try to creep in.

"Thanks, Mr. Cooper!" Tommy said. "I feel way better already."

Mr. Cooper smiled. "You're on your way, Tommy. Remember, you have the power to control your thoughts and change how you feel. Just keep practicing these techniques, and you'll see amazing results."

Tommy headed out, his mind buzzing with the new technique he had learned. He felt more in control of his thoughts than ever before and couldn't wait to put the Power Flick into action the next time he stepped onto the football field.

Chapter 8: The Amazing Mind Shift

Mr. Cooper led Tommy into a new room that looked like a giant control centre. There were levers, dials, and buttons everywhere, all connected to a big screen on the wall.

"Did you know your mind stores memories in different ways?" Mr. Cooper asked with a smile. "And did you know that by changing how a memory looks, sounds, or feels, you can change how you feel about it?"

Tommy raised an eyebrow. "Really? How?"

Mr. Cooper walked over to the control panel and gestured to the screen. "Let's start with a memory you don't like. We'll change how it looks and sounds, and you'll see how that affects how you feel about it."

The screen flickered to life, showing Tommy's mistake on the football field—the moment he missed a save. Tommy felt that familiar sting of disappointment, but Mr. Cooper quickly moved to the control panel.

"First, let's adjust the brightness," Mr. Cooper said. He turned the dial, and the screen dimmed, making the image of the missed save less intense. "Notice how it doesn't seem as bright or overwhelming."

"Yes, Tommy said, it's not as in my face anymore."

"Now, let's change the sound," Mr. Cooper continued, moving another lever. The sound of the ball hitting the net became silly, almost like a cartoon sound, instead of the loud thud that Tommy remembered. "Does that make it feel different?"

Tommy giggled. "That sounds funny now. It's not so serious!"

"Exactly!" Mr. Cooper said, smiling. "Now, let's shrink the image. Watch as the mistake gets smaller and smaller."
Tommy watched in amazement as the image of him missing the save shrank, becoming tiny on the screen, almost like a little dot in the distance. "Wow, it's so small now."

"See how changing the way a memory looks and sounds can make it feel less powerful?" Mr. Cooper asked. "This is what we call 'sub modalities.' You can change the details of a memory—like its brightness, size, or sound—to change how it affects you."

Tommy was amazed. "So, I can make a bad memory feel less bad just by changing how it looks in my mind?"

"Correct!" Mr. Cooper said. "You're in control. The next time you think about a memory that bothers you, try adjusting its brightness, size, or sound. You'll be surprised at how much it can change how you feel about it."

Tommy grinned, feeling empowered. "It's just a memory now! I don't have to feel bad about it anymore."

"That's correct, Mr Cooper replied. Memories don't have to control you. You have the power to change how you think about them."

Tommy felt a new sense of freedom. He realised that he didn't have to carry the weight of his past mistakes with him. By changing how he viewed them, he could let go of the negative feelings and move forward with more confidence.

As Mr Cooper led Tommy away, Tommy was already thinking about how he could use the sub modalities technique the next time he felt disappointed or frustrated. He knew he had the tools to change his memories and his feelings, and that made him feel stronger than ever before.

Chapter 9: From Small Steps to Big Wins

Mr. Cooper led Tommy into a room filled with a giant magnifying glass and a telescope. "Sometimes, we get stuck on small problems, and they can feel huge, like the biggest thing in the world," Mr. Cooper said. "But if we zoom out and look at the bigger picture, we can see things more clearly."

Tommy looked at the tools in the room, curious. "What do you mean by zoom out?"

Mr. Cooper smiled. "Great question! Let's think about your football match. Sometimes, when we focus too much on one mistake, it can feel like it's the only thing that matters. But if we zoom out and look at the whole game, we see that one mistake doesn't define us."

He guided Tommy to the telescope and adjusted it to show the whole game. On the screen, Tommy could now see the entire match—his great saves, his teammates, and the fun he had. The missed save seemed much smaller in the bigger picture.

"See?" Mr. Cooper said. "When you zoom out, that one mistake looks so much smaller, right?"

Tommy nodded, his shoulders relaxing. "Yeah, now it feels like it doesn't matter as much. The whole game was bigger than just that one moment."

"Bingo!" Mr. Cooper said. "That's called 'chunking up'—when we focus on the bigger picture. It helps us see problems in a new way."

Tommy grinned. "That really helps! It's like the mistake was just a small part of something much bigger."

"You've got it" Mr. Cooper replied. "Now, let's try 'chunking down.'"

Tommy was curious. "What's chunking down?" "Well," Mr. Cooper explained, "chunking down means focusing on the smaller steps that can help you improve. Instead of looking at the whole game, we zoom in on tiny things you can work on, like you're positioning or staying focused even after a mistake."

Mr. Cooper pointed to a smaller screen that zoomed in on Tommy's previous save attempts, showing little details where Tommy could adjust his position to make a better save. It was like seeing the game piece by piece.

Tommy thought for a moment. "So, I don't have to fix everything all at once. I can just focus on one small thing at a time?"

"That's the way!" Mr. Cooper said. "It's all about focusing on the little steps. Every small improvement counts and helps you get better."

Tommy smiled. "I can do that! I'll focus on the small things, like my positioning, and not worry about fixing everything at once."

Mr. Cooper nodded. "That's the spirit! By zooming out, you can see the bigger picture and feel good about your progress. And by zooming in, you can focus on the small steps that lead to big success."

Tommy was starting to feel confident. Whether it was zooming out to see the whole game or zooming in on small improvements, he now had a way to tackle challenges without feeling overwhelmed.

"I get it now," Tommy said, smiling. "It's all about focusing on the right things—whether it's the big picture or the little details."

"That's the key," Mr. Cooper said, grinning. "And remember, you don't have to do everything at once. Small changes add up to big results over time."

Tommy walked out of the room, feeling ready for anything. He knew how to take a step back and see things from a different point of view, and how to focus on small, manageable steps to keep getting better. With these new tools, he felt ready to face any challenge that came his way.

Chapter 10: The Funny Voice Trick

Mr. Cooper grinned mischievously. "What if we could make your negative thoughts sound so ridiculous, that they couldn't bother you anymore?"

Tommy raised an eyebrow. "How can we do that?"

Mr. Cooper smiled. "It's easier than you think. We can change the way your thoughts sound. You know how when you hear something funny, you can't help but laugh?"

"Yeah, Tommy said, when something's silly, it just makes you giggle."

"That's right!" Mr. Cooper said, his eyes twinkling. "Now imagine, just for a moment, that you have a voice inside your head that tells you, 'You're not good enough!'"

Tommy frowned, thinking about the mean voice that sometimes popped up in his head when he made a mistake.

"That voice can sound so serious and convincing, can't it?" Mr. Cooper said. "But what if we changed it into something really silly?"

Tommy's eyes widened. "Like what?"

Mr. Cooper pointed to a screen, and Tommy saw a big bubble with the words "You're not good enough!" floating inside. "Imagine that phrase coming from a silly, squeaky chipmunk voice, like this— 'You're not good enough!'" Mr. Cooper said, putting on a high-pitched, squeaky chipmunk voice.

Tommy couldn't help but burst out laughing. The image of the chipmunk saying those words was just too funny.

"See?" Mr. Cooper said, smiling. "When you make a negative thought sound ridiculous, it loses all its power. That chipmunk voice couldn't make you feel bad, could it?"

Tommy shook his head, still laughing. "No way! That's so silly!"

Mr. Cooper grinned. "That's it! When you start hearing your negative thoughts in a silly voice, they start to sound funny and unimportant. The more ridiculous you make them, the less seriously they affect you."

Tommy thought for a moment. "So, if I ever hear that voice saying, 'You're not good enough!' again, I can just imagine it sounding like a goofy chipmunk, and it won't bother me?"

"Yep," Mr. Cooper said. "And you can get even more creative! What if you imagined the voice sounding like a cartoon character, or even like a robot saying it in a silly way?"

Tommy's eyes lit up with excitement. "I could make it sound like a funny robot! Or even like a pirate!"

Mr. Cooper chuckled. "There you go! The more creative you get with it; the less power those negative thoughts will have over you."

Tommy was starting to feel more confident. "I can't wait to try this next time I hear that voice in my head."

Mr. Coopers smile widened. "Remember, when you make your negative thoughts sound silly, they can't control you. You take back the power, and you get to choose how you respond."

Tommy was starting to understand. It wasn't just about fighting negative thoughts—it was about transforming them into something laughable and harmless. He felt lighter and more in control.

"Thanks, Mr. Cooper! This is awesome!" Tommy said, smiling.

Mr. Cooper winked. "I'm glad you think so. Now you have another tool to help you stay in control of your thoughts and feelings. Whenever something negative pops up, just turn it into something silly, and watch it lose all its power."

Tommy grinned. "I can't wait to try it! I'll make every negative thought sound so silly; it won't stand a chance!"

Chapter 11: You Are in Control

Mr. Cooper smiled. "Tommy, you've learned so much! Remember, you control your feelings. With these techniques, you can handle anything!"

Tommy clapped his hands together. "I feel ready for anything!"

Mr. Cooper beamed with pride. "The power is always with you. Whenever you face a challenge, you can use what you've learned to stay calm, focused, and confident."

Tommy thought about everything he had learned — the box technique to let go of bad feelings, reframing his thoughts, visualising success, and all the other tools that would help him grow. He felt stronger than ever, ready to face whatever came next.

Suddenly, Tommy was back in his room, as though nothing had happened. The Feeling Factory was still there, inside him — its colourful machines and tools waiting to be used whenever he needed them.

Tommy smiled to himself, feeling calm and empowered. No matter what happened next, he knew he had the tools to handle it.

As he grabbed his football boots, he didn't just feel ready for his next match — he felt ready for anything. And with a confident grin, he stepped out into the world, knowing he was in control.

Final Message to the Reader

You are in control of your feelings! Just like Tommy, you can change the way you think and feel using these powerful techniques.

Whenever you feel stuck, remember:

- See the bigger picture with Reframing
- Throw away bad feelings with The Magic Box Trick
- Use the power of imagination with Visualising
- The power of Anchoring those happy thoughts
- Change how memories look and sound with The Power Flick
- Change the sub – modalities with the Amazing Mind Shift
- Go from small steps to big wins when you Chunk up and down
- Make bad thoughts sound silly with The Funny Voice Trick

You are **STRONG**.

You are **CAPABLE**.

You can do **ANYTHING** you put your mind to!

This book is dedicated to Tommy Horne whose journey inspired this story. May you always believe in your strength, your dreams and your magic

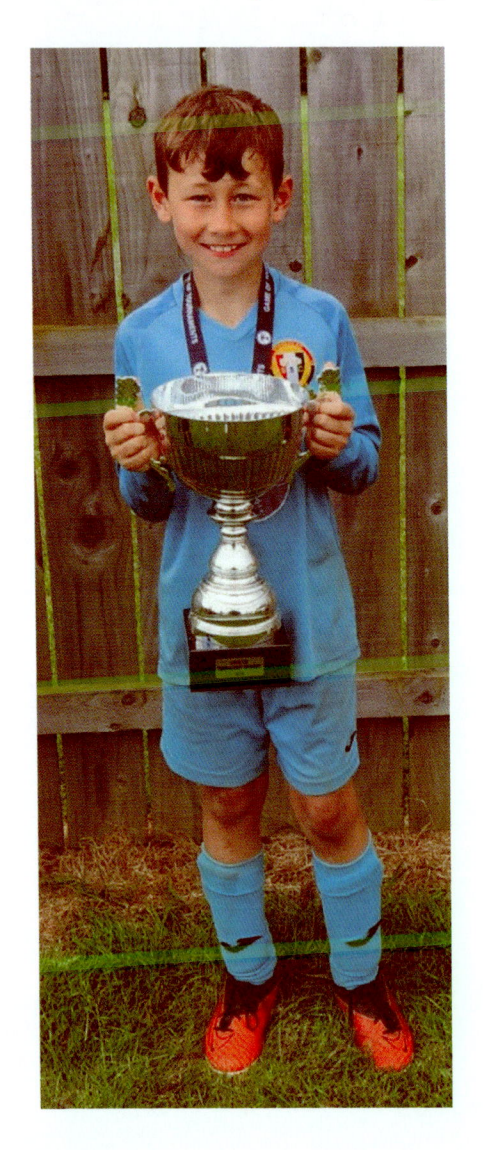

About the Author

Chris Horne is a passionate mental health advocate and a Master Practitioner in Neuro-Linguistic Programming (NLP), working with both children and adults to help them understand and manage their emotions. His work focuses on giving people the tools to build confidence, resilience, and emotional wellbeing.

Blending psychology with storytelling, Chris brings powerful mental techniques to life through engaging, imaginative journeys. *Tommy and the Feeling Factory* is his first children's book, inspired by the belief that emotional awareness should be fun, empowering, and accessible for every child.

Chris is the co-founder of **Positive Mindset Coaching Ltd**, a company dedicated to helping individuals unlock their true potential through emotional wellbeing, resilience and positive mindset training.

Printed in Great Britain
by Amazon